RAMAYAN AN EPIC TALE

FROM CHILD'S PERSPECTIVE

RIVA GANDHI

notionpress.com

INDIA · SINGAPORE · MALAYSIA

ISBN 979-8-88909-953-6

Contents

# Royal Family

The Solar Dynasty (Surya Vansha) began with Vaivaswata Manu who was the son of Sun-God. Manu was also the first ruler of mankind. His eldest son Ikshvaku built the city of Ayodhya on the banks of holy river Sarayu.

With passage of time, the Solar Dynasty became famous with name of Raghu Dynasty by virtue of the Sarva Dakshina Yagya (giving away one's wealth in charity).

King Dashrath was the grandson of Emperor Raghu and had inherited all the virtues of his great ancestors and had many qualities of his own. He was so noble that he had no enemies. He was a very wealthy king and has three queens.

# The childhood

King Dashrath had only one regret, that he was not blessed with a son. So, the famous Rishi Shringa was invited to perform the Putrakameshti yagya to beget the son. The auspicious sacrifice was performed when Sage Shringa offered oblations to the holy fire, the fire God Agni appeared.

The fire God held the bowl of kheer to Dashrath and asked to distribute it to his wives. He called for his three queens at once. King Dashrath gave half of the kheer to queen Kaushalya. Then he gave one of the parts to queen Kaikeyi, then queen Kaushalya and queen Kaikeyi gave their half parts of kheer to queen Sumitra. Soon after having the kheer, the three queens had conceived. There was joy and happiness all around.

King Dashrath was overjoyed. He felt as if he had got everything in the world. He thanked all the gods in the heaven. All the Queens were overjoyed and glad at heart since they became pregnant. They were all very happy. In due course, the sun, moon, and the stars align themselves in auspicious positions. It was the ninth day of the sacred month of Chaitra. The sun was in the middle of the sky as it was noon time. It was neither too hot, not too cold. A cool soft and fragrance breeze was blowing. The three queens bore four lovely boys. Thirteen days after the birth of the boys, the naming ceremony was performed by Sage Vasishta.

- The eldest son was named 'Ram' as he was very embodiment of joy and bliss for the whole universe.

- The second son was named 'Bharat' as he sustained and supported the universe.

- The third son was named 'Lakshman' as he was abode of noble virtues, the beloved of Lord Ram and the base of the universe.

- The fourth son was named 'Shatrughan' as he was destroyer of enemies.

Kaushalya gave birth to Ram, Kaikeyi to Bharat and Sumitra to twin boys Lakshman and Shatrughan. The whole palace was filled with laughter and joy.

With their four parent the boys grew up in the palace. But as soon as the four boys reached adolescence, they were invested with the secret thread. With their Guru Vasishta the princes went to the hermitage for a life of simplicity and learning. They slept on the floor, ate bland food, observed the discipline of the hermitage, and helped in daily chorus.

With their clever minds and quick intellect, they soon mastered all the branches of the knowledge.

Among the skills they learned at the gurukul was archery. When the education of four princes came to an end. Sage Vashistha informed King Dashrath that they should return to the palace. Sumanthra was sent to receive the four sons. He took royal robes for the princes. Now the four princeses clad themselves in the royal robes which had been brought by Sumanthra, they also put on the crowns and other ornaments. The swift horses soon reached the city of Ayodhya, the people were waiting for the glimpse of four princes. The whole city was nicely decorated and there was a great rejoicing and happiness everywhere.

Ram Lakshman Accompanies Vishwamitra

King Dashrath was happy to see his four sons grow up as a violent, virtuous, brave, and amiable person.

Meanwhile in a hermitage deep in the forest lived Sage Vishwamitra, practicing austerities in secluded and sacred retreat. However, demons like Subahu and Marich began to disturb his prayers and rituals.

One day, Vishwamitra arrived at the court of Ayodhya. Dashrath bowed down before the wise sage and welcomed him then he bathed the feet of the sage. King Dashrath with folded hands asked the sage the purpose of his visit and assured him that his command will be obeyed. Vishwamitra said that "I am performing yagya, two powerful demons, Marich and Subahu defile it by showering blood and bones on the sacred fire". He said that my fears will come to an end if you send your eldest son Ram and his younger brother Lakshman with me. Dashrath's heart raced, and his face grew pale. He stood speechless and stunned. Dashrath pleaded to Vishwamitra to change his mind. He said that my sons are dearer to me than my life itself ask me for anything land, cattle, wealth, treasure. I am ready to give you without a moment's hesitation. Sage Vishwamitra was pained to hear Dasharatha's outburst it was then Sage Vasishta interrupted, he said that let them go! they are old enough to do this task. Dashrath agreed and the two boys were called to the court. King Dashrath then clasped his sons to his bosom and ask them to look after each other. Then Ram and Lakshman went to the palace of the Queen's to take their blessings. They were glad to go for an adventure.

Vishwamitra along with Ram and Lakshman began the journey having crossed the river Ganga the three

 RAMAYAN - An Epic Tale

made their difficult way through a dense forest known as Dandaka Forest. For a long time, people lived there happily till Tadaka and her sons, Marich and Subahu changed it into a dreadful wilderness. On the way, they saw Tadka who hearing their voice charged upon them, but Ram was ready. With a single well aimed arrow Ram killed Tadka.

Vishwamitra applauded Rams valour, then the sage took the boys to his hermitage. He gave them various kinds of weapons and give them many fruits and bulbs to eat. At the break of dawn, Ram assured the sage to perform the sacrifice without any fear of interference, Vishwamitra and other sages started offering oblations to the holy fire. Suddenly demon Subahu reached there with his army, but Ram was ready for him. He aimed for Subahu, the demon leader attacking him with an arrow of fire. Thus, Subha the son of Tadka was killed.

Tadka's other son Marich was disturbed of his mother's death and decided to quit the path of injustice. He went too far off land and started to meditate in a cave. Meanwhile, for a few days, Ram and Lakshman remained at the ashram, listening to the Legends and tales of yore.

Ahalya redeemed

One day Sage Vishwamitra expressed his desire to Ram and Lakshman for going to Mithila and seek blessings of Lord Shiva's bow (Dhanush). Ram being a staunch devotee of lord Shiva, he was very excited and felt blessed with the opportunity to seek blessings of Lord Shiva's bow Dhanush. Sage Vishwamitra, Ram, and Lakshman started their journey to Mithila (also known as Janakpuri). While going through the jungle, they came across a deserted ashram. (A place where a sage lived with his wife and children). Ram was curious to know about the deserted ashram in detail, then Sage Vishwamitra told him the story. How Gautam Rishi used to live with his wife Ahalya. Lord Brahma created the most beautiful woman Ahalya who was married to Gautam Rishi. They had a son named Shatananda and used to live in peace and were happy. Then one day. Gautam Rishi went to have a bath in the river. While he was away, Lord Indra disguised himself as Gautam Rishi and entered the hut of Ahalya. While Indra was turning back, he saw Gautam Rishi right in front of him. Gautam Rishi was so angry that he cursed Indra to become a eunuch. He cursed his wife Ahalya that she will be turned into a rock. As soon as he said that he realised his mistake that he cursed his wife, she was innocent. But as he could not take his curse back, he changed it so that one day the Suryavanshi warrior would free her from the curse. Then Ram said that "I don't know whether I am that Suryavanshi warrior, but if I am I have taken too long to come". Many villagers tried to stop Ram not to enter Sage Gautam's abandoned Ashram. Shatananda too arrived.

As Ram set foot in the hermitage the curse was lifted and Ahalya stood before him in all beauty. True penance has such powers. Then Gautam Rishi apologised to Ahalya and seeked her forgiveness. Then the three continued the journey to Mithila.

Sita's Swayamvar

Once reaching Mithila they decided to rest at sage Yagyavlkya's ashram. They met Yagyavlkya and his two wives. They also met Gurumata Gargi who asked a few questions to Ram, who confidently answered the questions, Gurumata was impressed with Ram and was surprised to see all the good qualities in one person. Till then King Janak was also pleased with the arrival of Vishwamitra along with Ram and Lakshman in Mithila.

The news of their arrival also spread like wildfire through Janakpuri, the next day two princes with the permission of their guru went to gather flowers for morning prayers. In the garden they so lovely bunch of flowers the songs of koel, parrot added music to the air and graceful peacock's dance to the tune. amid the garden was a lovely lake with limpid clear water where lotuses bloomed. Just as the Princes where busy gathering flowers Sita, daughter of King Janak came to the garden, she was on her way to the temple of Parvati near the lake accompanied by group of girls singing sweetly. While Sita was in the temple one of her friends stayed behind to admire the flowers suddenly, she saw Ram and Lakshman thrilled at their sight she rushed to tell Sita and her companions.

As her friend described the two princes, Sita felt a strange longing in her heart. But soundlessly she followed where her companions led her. As Sita was walking the jingle-jangle of the bangles and the soft tinkling of anklets and girdle bells attracted Ram's attention. He turned towards the sound and stood spellbound when he gazed at Sita. He was filled with rapture by her beauty but could not utter a word. At last, he controlled his emotions and said to Lakshman that this surely must be King Janak's daughter. She has come to worship goddess Gauri. While he was speaking Rams eyes followed Sita. Sita was looking around the garden in her shy timid way. When Sita at last caught sight of the princes she felt elated overcome with the emotion she closed her eyelids capture the captivating image in her mind.

Sita's friends realise that she was disturbed. Sita returned to the temple and fell at the feet of the idol of goddess Gauri and said that you know mother my hearts longing, Please bless me, the idol seemed to smile, and the garland fell from goddess Gauri's neck to Sita. Then Sita and her friends returned joyfully who the palace reassured by the divine proclamation. Meanwhile Ram and Lakshman too returned to their ashram. The day past in prayer and stories from thescriptures.

Finally, the day arrived for Janak's daughter Sita Swayamvar. Many valiant princes and kings from all over the world were invited to the Swayamvar to win the hand of Sita. Janak welcomed them and showed them around and told the tale of the bow. He said that this enormous bow belongs to Lord Shiva once when Sita was small, I was amazed to see that she could lift it since then I woved that I would marry her to someone who could lift this mighty bow. Then Sita arrived with her friends bedecked and bejewelled like beauty personified.

The bow was big, and it took the strength of several men to bring it to the arena. The announcement made the nobles eager to try their hands. One by one they came forward although they exerted all their strength, they could not even move the bow.

Among the kings and princes, Ravan the king of Lanka was also present. Ravan was filled with arrogance and overconfidence. He tried to lift bow with all his strength and power but was not able to lift the bow. Alas! Ravan the greatest devotee of Lord Shiva was not able to lift the bow and gave up. He felt very disgusted and returned to Lanka at once. The other kings and princes present there wanted to declare a war.

Suddenly Vishwamitra along with Ram and Lakshman stepped in the assembly. Vishwamitra said that whoever wanted to fight can have a war with Ram and Lakshman. The whole assembly was quiet. But king Janak was miserably pained and said that I think there is no hero on this earth who can lift this bow and win my lovely daughter Sita. After Janak uttered these words, the whole assembly was quiet but Lakshman was filled with anger. He said, "In an assembly where anyone from Raghu dynasty is present no one should make such statement. Ram pacified Lakshman, sage Vishwamitra said "Up Ram, lift the bow of Shiva and relieve Janak from all his anguish". On hearing his gurus' words Ram touched the holy feet of Vishwamitra. Ram moved towards the bow then he meditated on Lord Shiva. He lifted the bow effortlessly as if it were a garland of flowers. He grasped the string and drew it tight then he broke the bow in two halves. It produced a great noise like thundering the earth shook all the people were gasped.

Sita face was lit with joy and Lakshman's with pride. Sita put the victory garland around Rams neck. There was rejoicing everywhere. At last a worthy suitor had been found for lovely Sita.

# The Wedding

During the uproar, Sage Parshuram arrived there he came there thundering and roaring with a bow on one shoulder and the battle axe on the other. All the kings and princes trembled in fear. Parshuram spoke in harsh words and addressed to king Janak "Who has broken this bow? Show him at once or I will destroy your whole Kingdom". Janak was too terrified to reply. Then Ram spoke with folded hands "My Lord the one who broke the bow is none but a servant of yours". Parshuram was furious and replied that the one who broke this bow is my enemy and not a servant. Then Lakshman said "I have broken many bows in my childhood, but you never got so angry. Why are you so fond of this particular bow? "Parshuram now grew more furious at Lakshman he was about to slay him with his axe. Just in time Vishwamitra intervened and stopped Parshuram. Ram said, "I didn't have any intention of breaking the bow however wanted to protect the dignity and clear the misconception about the bow and save King Janak and her daughter Sita from the false allegations levelled by all the King's present in the assembly".

Ram's word impressed sage Parshuram. He then gave his bow and said this bow was given to my father by Lord Vishnu if you string this bow, I will bow to you as the avatar of Lord Vishnu. Ram took the bow and arrow from Parshuram. In the twinkling of an eye, he strung the bow and set the arrow to it. Then Ram askedParshuram where to release it? Parshuram bowed to Ram and asked to release it in the correct direction. Then Parshuram realised that his time was over and went back to perform the penance.

The God showered flowers on Lord Ram. Happiness descended in every heart. Janak sent messengers to Ayodhya. King Janak the next day invited Ram and Lakshman for lunch.

Meanwhile when the messengers reached Ayodhya, they gave king Dashrath the letter given by King Janak. Dashrath's home minister read out the letter allowed which said that "Ram has won the hand of Sita by breaking Lord shiva's bow and wants the blessings and approval of yours and the three Queens for the wedding ceremony"

The king and his noble courtiers were delighted to hear the feat performed by the young Ram. The three Queens Kaushalya, Kaikeyi, Sumitra, Bharat, and Shatrughan rejoiced. But according to the tradition of Ayodhya the Queens could not attend the wedding of their sons. The Queens were disheartened but soon accepted the reality and got busy in the wedding preparations.

Dashrath proceeded to Mithila for the wedding ceremony. He took with him abandoned riches and precious jewels. The sages accompanied the king

   RAMAYAN - An Epic Tale

on their glorious chariots. After a long journey the wedding party reached Janakpuri. King Janak welcome Dashrath and his men with open arms. After having a sumptuous meal everyone went to have rest.

Bharat and Shatrughan rushed to meet Ram and Lakshman. The next day was fixed for the wedding. Ram looked resplendent in the bright wedding garments and ornaments on his dark swarthy form. While attending one of the ritual Dashrath was impressed with the depth of knowledge and behaviour of Sita's sisters. A thought came in his mind of proposing the marriage of Lakshman, Bharat and Shatrughan with King Janak and his younger brother Kushadhwaj's daughters. He was very excited, and he expressed his thought to guru Vashistha. He was very much pleased with his suggestion. Then guru Vashistha asked Dashrath to express his desire to king Janak. King Janak and King Kushadhwaj were happy to hear the marriage proposal and their joy grew no bound.

Bharat to Mandavi, Lakshman to Urmila and Shatrughan to Shrutakirti.

The bride grooms and brides were led to the wedding mandap, family priest Vashistha and Shatananda performed all the religious rites and ceremonies according to their family customs. Janak and Sunaina, Kushadhwaj and Chandrabhaga washed the bridegrooms' feet with scented water.

Ram then applied vermillion powder on Sita's head followed by Bharat, Lakshmanan and Shatrughan to their respective brides.

The four princeses were married according to the prescribed ceremony. There was a sumptuous wedding feast with a delicious array of dishes. The wedding party was coaxed to stay on for several days after the wedding ceremony. Precious gifts were given by the two saintly brothers to their four daughters out of sheer love for them. Now came the very difficult time for king Janak and Kushadhwaj as they had to part ways from their daughters. At the end after the bidai everyone descended to Ayodhya.

Ram's coronation

Meanwhile in Ayodhya the queen mothers prepared for the welcome in the traditional manner. The newly married couples were welcomed with great pomp. Later, King Dashrath described the wedding rituals in detail to the enraptured queens.

The days passed in happiness, success and prosperity flowed into Ayodhya like bounteous rivers. One day while king Dashrath was in his court one of the ministers said that "Your Highness, Your crown is askew". Dasharatha asked for the mirror to adjust his crown. when he saw his own reflection in the mirror, he felt that his hairs were growing grey. He heard his own voice saying make Ram the king of Ayodhya.

The thought filled his heart with joy. Meanwhile, Bharat and Shatrughan had went to visit their grandfather Ashwapati to Kekaya. Meanwhile Dashrath decided to visit his guru Vashistha at once. Vashistha was glad to hear the King's intention. He advised Dashrath to convey meeting of the Rajya Sabha to seek its approval. Dashrath with his Guru's blessing called for Rajya Sabha at once. The whole assembly of Rajya Sabha of the elite declared with one voice that Ram should be coronated as he was the very embodiment of virtue and valour.

Having sought the unanimous approval of the Rajya Sabha without even a single dissenting note, King Dashrath asked his home minister Sumanthra to fetch Ram who was not aware of all these happenings. Ram came and bowed to his father. The King embraced him and having seated him on the throne besides him spoke out "Dear Son! I have grown old and have enjoyed my life as a man and as a king. Now there is nothing left for me to do except to crown you on the throne of our forefathers tomorrow itself.

Dasharath instructed Ram in connection with his coronation fixed for the next day sage Vashistha who was well versed in the Vedas and knew many sacred spells. Vashistha went in Ram and Sita's chamber and instructed them to keep fast and follow some rituals. Ram and Sita practiced penance that night they chanted the secret mantaras and slept on grass spread on the floor as advised by the sage.

Meanwhile there was great rejoicing all over Ayodhya as the ministers and citizens prepared for the jubilant function.

Manthara conspires with Kaikeyi

Now in the palace of Kaikeyi there was a mischief afoot, she had an evil-minded maid Manthara. Manthara was a hunch-backed woman and Queen Kaikeyi's personal maid. Kaikeyi was accompanied by Manthara from her maternal home to Ayodhya after her marriage. The moment she heard about Rams coronation her mind was filled with rage and envy. Manthara decided she must act fast and upset all the plans. With a woebegone face and tears in her eyes she went to her mistress Kaikeyi. She noticed her glum face and asked her what was bothering her. Manthara refused to speak but sighed deeply. Manthara spoke aloud "A flood of misfortune is rising to ruin and drown you. King Dashratha has decided to make Ram the ruler of this land in the absence of your son Bharat". Kaikeyi was overjoyed and very much pleased to hear about Rams coronation. But Manthara said Ram is going to be coronated so Kaushalya, his mother is filled with pride, go and see how the city is rejoicing then you will know my woe. She continued her vile web further "Your son is away, and you are blind to the tricks the king is playing, all you do is lay on your quilted bed in comfort". Kaikeyi was filled with anger and wanted to punish Manthara badly.

But Manthara was an old, trusted retainer. So, Kaikeyi cushioned her harsh words with sweet talks. Kaikeyi loved Ram dearly and he too was affectionate to her. But Manthara continued from tomorrow your son Bharat will be a subject and a slave. Ram will get him killed you will be reduced to the status of a maid servant Kaushalya. Manthara's wicked plan worked and Kaikeyi was mesmerised into believing her cunning words. Like the malignant Saturn that cost its influence for long Manthara began to cast her shadow on the royal household. Now Kaikeyi sought Manthara's help that what she should do in the present circumstances. Manthara said don't you remember the incident you once told me? Kaikeyi was not able to recollect and ask Manthara to tell her.

She started telling her the story once there was a fierce battle between the gods and the demons. King Dashratha went to help indra and was accompanied by you. In the battle Dashratha fell to the ground unconscious and you quickly drove chariot away from the battlefield and saved his life. The king was very pleased and grateful and granted her 2 boons. Kaikeyi suddenly remembered the 2 boons. Manthara asked to follow her advice and it was the right time to ask for the 2 boons. She said that ask for the throne for your son and send Ram to exile for 14 years. Manthara now gave detailed instructions to Kaikeyi. Kaikeyi instantly entered the sulking room (a room which ladies of the royal family retired to express their resentment). She dressed herself in a dirty saree, she removed all her ornaments and jewels and scattered them on the floor. Then she stretched herself on the bare floor.

All around her in the palace in outside there was celebration and jubilation. In the evening when the King visited Kaikeyi's palace he was shocked to know that she was in the sulking room. Dashratha was surprised to see her dressing and appearance. The old and innocent king tried his best to know the reason for her grief. But Kaikeyi remained as mute as a statue. Then Dashrath said "I swear in the name of Ram that I will do whatever you desire". The moment king Dashrath swore by Ram, Kaikeyi felt convinced. She reminded Dashratha of the 2 boons. Then King Dashrath said "Oh! I truly had forgotten about them surely you can ask me for four instead of just two boons. Kaikeyi said "I have two wishes one is the coronation of my son Bharat as the King and my second wish is that Ram should live like aesthetic in the forest for 14 years. Hearing these words of wicked Kaikeyi, Dashratha turned pale, and wasp paralysed with horror. He fell down unconscious and kept repeating Ram's name.

Dashrath cried piteously all night long stricken with sorrow.

At daybreak the auspicious sounds of flute, lute and conch rang out at the gate. All the ministers were waiting for the king to start the coronation ceremony.

One of the ministers asked Sumanthra to call the king. As Sumanthra approached the kings chamber, he saw Dashrath in a hapless state.

Sumanthra was shocked and went to Kaikeyi who was standing nearby. Kaikeyi asked him to call Ram as the King wished to meet him. As Ram entered the chamber, he saw with awestruck and amazement his father lying on the bare floor in deep grief and anguish. He touched his fathers' feet and then stood with folded hands before and said to her "Mother what ails father?" Kaikeyi replied, "Your father had promised me to boons long ago which I demanded last night". She told him the two boons "My son Bharat should be crowned today and you should go to the forest for 14 years". Ram without any hesitation accepted the command. Kaikeyi was surprised at Rams willingness to go to the forest without any hesitation at all.

Ram happily said "The forest will be a good place for me to stay, I will meet the hermits there. My dear Bharat will get the kingdom. Everything is wonderful. Only one thing saddens me, father is grieving over such a trifle". Having touched his father and Kaikeyi's feet Ram went out of the chamber. Ram decided to seek leave of his mother before departing for the forest meanwhile the news spread like wildfire throughout the town. Ram went to Kaushalya's chamber; she had no idea that tide had turned and gifted him with new clothes and jewels.

Ram touched the feet of Kaushalya and said, "Give me blessings mother for I must start my journey at once I will obey my father's word and return after spending 14 years in the forest". Kaushalya was shocked and surprised she wanted to know who was responsible for the change of heart, but Ram did not reply. Sumanthra who had accompanied Ram told what happened. Kaushalya pulled herself together and reminded herself that Ram and Bharat were both dear to her. Just then Sita heard the news and rushed there. She sat by her mother-in-law with tears in her eyes.

Sita said if my Lord goes to the forest what should I do? I must go with him or else I will surely die. Kaushalya tried to pacify her and said the forest is no place for such a delicate girl. There are wild animals and also many powerful and evil demons that dwell there. Ram also tried to explain her, You have no idea how awful the jungle can be with rough plants, deep ravines, lofty mountains, and wild animals. There are man-eating demons.

Sita's eyes filled with tears, and she fell at the feet of Kaushalya. Ram realised that if he left Sita at home, she may not be able to live so he asked Sita to make preparations to leave at once for the woods. Ram and Sita took leave of Kaushalya and met Lakshman on the way. He had just heard the news unable to speak he stood before Ram with folded hands. Ram lifted him gently and said you must stay here and look after our parents Bharat and Shatrughan are away and father is aged and sorrowing. Ayodhya needs you now! Lakshman said don't abandon me no one matters to me more than you. All my relationships are centred in you. Ram clasped Lakshman to his bosom and asked him to take leave of his mother. When Lakshman went to take the blessings of Sumitra. Sumitra instructed Lakshman to take care of brother Ram and Sita and make sure they received less hardship in the forest. She further said that you have to ensure that Ram and Sita sleep peacefully at night. Lakshman bowed to her. Meanwhile Kaikeyi fetched hermits' robes and vessels and placed them before Ram, Lakshman and Sita. Clad in hermits robes the three went to meet Dashrath. He bid sad farewell to Ram, Lakshman and Sita. The king lay on the floor, his glory gone and his face showing a deep sense of anguish. He kept on uttering "Oh! Ram, Oh! Lakshman, Oh! Sita! and cried. As the three came out of the palace a huge crowd gathered at the gates of the palace. Instead

                                      RAMAYAN - An Epic Tale

of the joy of Rams coronation they were faced with sorrow of his banishment. The citizens of Ayodhya were crying bitterly due to the separation from their beloved Ram.

> राम कीन्ह चाहहिं सोइ होई।
> करै अन्यथा अस नहिं कोई ॥

The will of Shri Ram alone prevails,

There is no one else who can alter it.

> कोउ नृप होई हमै का हानि,
> चेरी छांडि कि होइब रानी.

Who becomes the king will make no difference to me.

I am a servant; can I be the queen!!

Ram's exile begins

Dashrath ordered Sumanthra follow them with theirchariots take them to the forest. Show them around and when he returned, he must bring the three back with him. Sumanthra rushed at once with a well fitted chariot and went to the outskirts of the city where threesome had reached. Sumanthra said to them "Please let me leave you up to the edge of the forest. The King has asked me to do so". The three obeyed their fathers wish and mounted on the chariot with hordes of citizens following them on the foot. Ram persuaded them to turn back but they insisted on following him. Then Ram decided to hold for the night by the banks of River Tamasa. Ram went for the evening prayers by the river side and decided to fast on the first night of their forest life. Lakshman spread some kusa grass on the ground for Ram and Sita to sleep. Tired after the long journey people also found refuge on the banks of the river and went to sleep. While Lakshman spent the night guarding everyone.

Before dawn Ram rose from his sleep and told Sumanthra the loving citizens of Ayodhya who have followed us are now asleep. They shall not let me go ahead if they wake up let's drive away now quietly, make sure the chariot leaves no tracks for them to follow. Sumanthra obeyed and drove the chariot in such a way that the tracks were overlapping and confusing.

In the morning when the people woke up, they could not see Ram, Lakshman or Sita and their chariot anymore. Hapless they returned to Ayodhya. Sumanthra drove the chariot far into the forest having crossed many streams. They finally reached the southern boundary of the Kosala country. Here Ram got down the chariot and saluted his motherland Ayodhya with great reverence. The chariot reached the banks of Holy Ganga. They bathed in the holy river and Ram told them many legends about Ganga while they rested on its bank. The news of their arrival reached Guha, the Chief of Nishad. Gathering gifts of the jungle like roots and fruits he came to meet Ram. Ram embraced Guha who said with folded hands "Feel perfectly at home in my Kingdom, Kindly spend 14 years with us". Ram kindly said "Brother I very well know how much you love me, but I am bound by my own vows. I must spend 14 years in the forest". After the evening prayers Ram retired, Lakshman sat at a distance with his bow and arrow aloft. Guha placed his trustworthy soldiers all around and sat beside Lakshman. The next morning after bathing Ram and Lakshman matted the hair on their head with the banyan sap.

Ram then asked Sumanthra to return to Ayodhya and take care of his father. Hearing this words Sumanthra could not control himself and started to

                    RAMAYAN - An Epic Tale

cry. Ram consoled him and asked to take care of the royal family. With heavy heart Sumanthra drove back to Ayodhya.

# Reaching Chitrakoot

Ram then went in search of boat to cross the Ganga; he met a boat man. Can you ferry us across, boatman? The reply was no. "No, I cannot do so I have heard about you and your prowess the dust of your feet turns the rock into Hermitage's wife. He continued my wooden boat is not as hard as a rock what if it turns into a woman? My boat is my life my livelihood I will be lost without it". But Ram insisted "But we must cross the river". The boatman said well in that case allow me to wash your feet. Ram smiled and agreed to his strange request. The ferryman bought a wood basin full of water. He washed Lord Ram's lotus feet with love and devotion. Having washed the holy feet of lord Ram, the boatman along with other members of family drank the same. Then the boatman gladly took the Lord across the Ganga's. The ferryman felt prostrate at Lord Ram's feet for his blessings. Sita took off her jewelled ring to give it to the boatman for his services. But he would not take it. He fell to Ram's feet and said "Oh Lord all my cravings have seized today. Your glorious visit has ended all my suffering and shortcomings". After that Ram made clay image of Shiv and prayed before it. Sita bowed to the celestial river Ganga and sought her blessings. Ram then asked Guha to return to his place. Then they visited the Hermitage of sage Bharadwaj. They were welcomed by everyone in the ashram. Ram enquired where they could live in peace and safety. The sage replied that chitrakoot would be the most ideal place for them.

Dashrath breathe his last

When Sumanthra returned to the palace all alone, he noticed that Dashrath was in grief. Dashrath was heartbroken and his health was badly affected. He then remarked "A son like Ram was neither born before nor will be born in future, I cannot live without him". All of a sudden, he remembered the curse inflicted upon him by a blind sage long long ago. he recalled the curse of Shravan and narrated it to Kaushalya. Long ago while I was out hunting, I mistook a young hermit for a fleeting deer and shot him with an arrow, he was Shravan Kumar the soul support of his blind aged parents. Shravan said to me with difficulty "Oh! king I was filling the pitcher for my parents. Now you must take this water to them and tell them of my death". Shravan Kumar then died instantly; I stood trembling. When I reached the tree under which his parents were sitting with the pitcher of water, I saw that the old blind parents sat there like two birds with broken wings. I fell at their feet and confessed how in my ignorance I had killed their son. The miserable parents were dumbstruck by my dreadful fate. The boy's parents were so devastated that they too decided to end their lives. But before they did so they cursed Dashrath "You too shall die grieving for your beloved son just as we have grieved in the death of ours". Dashrath realised that the curse of Shravan's parent was now upon him. Filled with deep agitation king Dashrath passed away with the name of his beloved son on his lips. The whole palace plunged into gloom. All the Queens were weeping bitterly, they fell to the body of the dead king praising him for his valour virtues name and fame. "Today the son of a solar race who was an embodiment of righteousness and piety has set".

Next day, an enlightened sage arrived in the palace. Sage Vashistha tried to disperse the gloom with the light of his wisdom play. The King's dead body was immersed in a boat full of oil till Bharat's arrival. Able bodied messengers who could run fast were sent to fetch Bharat and Shatrughan.

Bharat visits Ram in exile

Bharat had evil dreams that night. He saw in his dreams that some dear one has passed away. His fears were confirmed when the messenger from Ayodhya came. Bharat and Shatrughan started for Ayodhya. The city wore a deserted look Bharat hurried to the palace of Dashrath, but he was not to be seen anywhere. He asked Kaikeyi where his father, brothersRam and Lakshman and other Queens were. Kaikeyi quickly filled her eyes with false tears. My son, Your father enjoyed life and all its blessing profusely. He earned great name and fame. He lived a virtuous life and he has now gone to his heavenly abode.

On hearing this Bharat fell to the ground and wept bitterly like an orphan child in uncontrolled grief. Bharat then asked mother where is Ram? Now he is both father and preceptor to me. Kaikeyi narrated all that she had done. Bharat's grief knew no bounds he busted out "Murderer mother you've wrecked and ruined our family! You were blinded by greed. I shall destroy all my relationships with you". Shatrughan too burned with rage then too he kept quiet, but when he saw Manthara clad with rich clothes and heavy jewels, he lost his control. He kicked her so hard that her hunch and head were both broken. Then both Bharat and Shatrughan rushed to Kaushalya who was shabbily dressed. Bharat blamed himself for all the happenings. Kaushalya pacified him and asked not to blame himself. The two brothers cried inconsolably, and Kaushalya clasped them to her heart when she began to weep Bharat becalmed her. The next day Bharat and Shatrughan performed the funeral rites of their great father. After a few days the ministers called the assembly, everyone said that Bharat should be crowned the king. Even Kaushalya said to him"You are the sole refugee of the family now, with Ram in forest and King in heaven".

Bharat said with folded hands "It is my final decision not to accept the crown. All of us will go to the forest we will bring brother Ram back who alone shall be crowned the king". Everyone applauded Bharat's suggestion. The people of Ayodhya, Saints and sages followed Bharat to the forest to fetch Ram. A huge army marched to protect them from wild animals. Avast cloud of dust cover the sky bird took to flight in panic. Lakshman climbed up a tree and was alarmed to see Bharat with a huge

     RAMAYAN - An Epic Tale

army advancing towards their hut. He got ready to fight. But Ram told Lakshman that Bharath was coming to take them back. Having halted the army at some distance Bharat, Shatrughan, Vasishta and Sumanthra went near the hut of Ram. Lakshman tried to stop Bharat from advancing towards the hut, On the other hand Bharat was very happy to see Lakshman. In anger Lakshman said "You have taken everything away from brother Ram, I won't allow you to go to the hut". Bharat explained Lakshman that "I'm here to take brother back and not to fight with him". Lakshman realised his mistake and apologised to Bharat. Lakshman then took Bharat and others to the hut seeing brother Ram, Bharat felt on his feet, Ram raised Bharat up and clasped him to his bosom. it was a sight for sore eyes. It was a scene of great emotional reunion. Bharat led a huge assembly including his brother Shatrughan, the Queens and Guru Vashistha followed by the ministers and soldiers. When Ram saw them, he greeted each one with warm affection. Ram saw that the three Queens were dressed in white and was stricken with grief. Then Bharat said "Father is no more. My dear brothers come back to the Kingdom, Lord Ram the throne belongs to you". Ram, Lakshman and Sita were devastated to hear of their father's death. Ram and Lakshman performed the tarpan in Mandakini River". While Janak heard all the news, he mounted on his chariot and came to Chitrakoot. Janak paid his respect to Guru Vashistha, Ram and Lakshman bowed to the seers from Ayodhya. Sorrowful speeches and sad sights drowned the assembly in a sea of grief at the loss of King Dashrath. Bharat asked him to come back to Ayodhya and rule the Kingdom. Ram replied "Dearbrother, I can never disobey my father's words, Shatrughan is there to help you rule over the Kingdom". If I fail to fulfil our fathers desire, I cannot find contentment even in the position of the whole world. Janak and Bharat had to agree with him. Bharat replied "You are my father and my God; your wish is sacred to me." Kindly give me your wooden sandals that shall rule over Ayodhya till your return. So be it replied Ram. Bharat then turned back towards Ayodhya with the people and the army. After reaching Ayodhya, Vashistha chose auspicious time and date for the coronation. Bharat then placed his brother's sandal on the throne and said "Let the sandals of my brother represent his reign over the kingdom of Ayodhya". Bharat cast off his royal robes and jewels and decided to live like a hermit. He made a simple hut of leaves and twigs near Ayodhya and wore clothes of bark. He gathered his hair in a metered knot and slept on the bed of kusha grass. His spartan lifestyle made him lean yet his face radiated spiritual strength.

Shurpanakha humiliated

Ram then suggested to Lakshman "I think we should move from Chitrakoot too many people know that we leave here". The three of them went to Sage Atri's ashram where they received a warm welcome. Sage Atri's wife Anasuya gave a wonderful present to Sita. Anasuya said "These are divine clothes and jewels that will remain fresh and new forever throughout your long stay in the jungle". Anasuya also gave Sita a lot of advice on the duties of a wife. Then Ram, Sita and Lakshman bid farewell to Sage Atri and Anasuya and made their way to the Hermitage of Sage Agastya. Ram had a purpose for meeting Agastya. The three bowed to the learned sage. Ram then said "Please guide me tell me the way to slay the demons the foes of hermit". Agastya replied "There is a charming holy spot called Panchvati in the Dandak forest". When they reached Panchvati, they fell in love with the place. It was a beautiful place near the River Godavari rich with fragment, lucius fruits and abundant water. It was here that Ram met Jatayu the king of vultures. Ram got to know that Dashrath and Jatayu were old friends. Ram built a bond of friendship with him. Ram and Sita lived happy and peaceful life in the cottage of Panchvati. They were lovingly served by Lakshman.

Suddenly, Ravan's sister Shurpanakha happened to come there. Her nails were as big as a winnowing fan. She was horribly ugly. When she was passing by Panchvati, all of sudden she heard voices as she stopped to see who was there, she was amazed by the glowing image of Ram and immediately fell in love with him. But she knew how horrible she looked so she magically transformed herself into a beautiful young woman and approached Ram. She said "There is no man like you and no woman like me. God has planned our match with a lot of thought, I have searched the whole worldwide, but I haven't found a man good enough for me". Ram told Shurpanakha that he was already married and pointed towards Sita. So, she proposed to Lakshman who was equally handsome. Shurpanakha asked Lakshman to marry her without any further delay. Lakshman exclaimed me "Oh! no I'm like his servant, my brother is more valiant than I am". Realising that both Ram and Lakshman were joking she became furious. She changed back to her original form and charged at Sita, I shall kill you and eat you up, You ugly model. When Shurpanakha spoke these words, Lakshman saw that Sita was very frightened so he took out his dagger and cut off Shurpanakha's nose. Screaming and yelling in pain he sent her scurrying back in humiliation into the deep forest.

Ram faces Khar and Dushan

She went to her to stepbrother Khar and Dushan. Shurpanakha explained "Look at me my brave brothers! Ram and Lakshman have committed such crimes on me even though you're still alive moreover they are dwelling fearlessly in your domain. Shurpanakha told them in detail her version of the incident. Khar called their army together for attack. Huge ugly monsters of various shapes and sizes appeared. They had strange animals on the vehicles in were armed with dreadful weapons. They raised such a storm with her march in the skies that Ram was alerted. He told Lakshman "That an army of demons is approaching, quickly take Sita to the cave and be on the guard". Lakshman led Sita to the cave in the mountain. Ram was ready with his bow and arrow aloft, the battle began. The constant stream of deadly arrows spread from Ram's arrow brought down warrior's chariots elephants and horses. Ram killed Khar and Dushan. Sita and Lakshman return from the cave after the demon army had been killed. Lakshman embraced Ram and rejoiced that single handed, he had given safety to the Saints and sages dwelling in that forest. Meanwhile when Shurpanakha realised that Khar and Dushan were killed she decided to go the powerful king of Lanka, Ravan.

Ravan approaches Marich

As Shurpanakha visited Lanka, she ran to meet Ravan who was sitting in his court. As she appeared closer to the throne Ravan and the courtiers noticed that she was wounded and bleeding. Ravan was enraged when he saw his sister in such state and ask her the reason behind it. Shurpanakha told him in detail her version of the incident. The sons of Dashrath, the King of Ayodhya are roaming in the forest they look like young boys but have immense strength they've promised the sages that they will kill all the demons, the handsome youth is called Ram and with him is his wife and brother she concluded. Someone in the court said why did you not call for help. She replied sadly "I did Khar and Dushan came with their armies to help me, but Ram killed them all". Ravan had been listening to her lament absentmindedly so far but now he was alert. Ravan consoled Shurpanakha and assured her as much as he could be by boasting about his strengths and might. But when he retired to his palace, he spent a sleepless night.

Ravan decided that there was no time for thought and he had to act at once. He decided to abduct Sita. He was stopped by Mandodri his wife and Vibhishana his brother who were very kind. But Ravan paid no heed to their advice. Alone he mounted his chariot and drove to the seashore where Marich lived as Sage. Ravan's visit surprised Marich, he then unfolded his plan to Marich. He continued you are capable of changing your format, you must disguise yourself as a golden deer and meanwhile I will abduct Sita. Marich refused and said "Oh! Ten-headed one! Though he may look like an ordinary man Ram is not the person you should antagonise. Marich recalled his earlier encounter with Ram. He said, long ago he had come to the sage Vishwamitra hermitage, with just one arrow he hit me so hard that I was hurled a hundred yojanas away. No good will come out of making any enemy of Ram. Marich shivered with fright at the very thought of confronting Ram again. He said to Ravan "Think about it he is the one who killed Subahu and my Mother Tadka, he also killed Khar and Dushan he broke the mighty bow of Shiva can he be an ordinary mortal? Go home if you wish well for your people.

Ravan was enraged hearing the advice of Marich. Marich was not truly on the horns of the dilemma, he thought if I argue anymore Ravan will kill me if I do as he says I will die at Ram's hand either way doom is certain. Having made his choice, he decided to follow Ravan.

> **रघुकुल रीत सदा चली आई, प्राण जाए पर वचन न जाई**

In the family of the Raghus, there has always been the tradition of upholding the truth,

Even at the cost of one's life!!

> **धीरज धर्म मित्र अरु नारी, आपद काल परिखिअहिं चारी**

Fortitude, piety, friend and wife are put to test only during adversity!!

Sita's abduction

Ravan led Marich to the dense dark forest. Marich used his miraculous powers and in the twinkling of an eye turned into a marvellous golden deer studded with gems. There he started prancing around Sita attracting her attention with a slender neck, gentle eyes in the body that glowed softly.

"What a beautiful deer! Sita said, Bring him to meet my Lord". Lakshman warned that the deer might be some demon when Ram went ahead to capture him. Ram asked him not to worry and instructed Lakshman to take care of Sita as there are hordes of demons roaming in the jungle. Ram took up his bow and arrows and set out to hunt for the golden deer. Marich took Ram so far out so that the Ravan could get plenty of time in opportunity to kidnap Sita. Meanwhile, Ram immediately sensed something unusual and shot an arrow that pierced right through the deer's heart. The deer collapsed and his form change to that of Marich. Ram was shocked to see him but before breathing his last, Marich still up to his old tricks cried out in a voice like that of Ram "O! Sita, O! Lakshman" At the hut Sita heard Ram's voice crying out for Lakshman. Sita was scared and worried she said to Lakshman "Hurry up and go your brother is in

RAMAYAN - An Epic Tale

a great danger". But Lakshman knew that Ram cannot be in trouble and said "It's not possible, my brother cannot be in a trouble". But Sita did not listen to Lakshman's calm response. She insisted he should go to once. Lakshman realised that he was being forced to go in search of Ram so he decided to go in search of Ram, but he was alsoworried about Sita safety so before leaving the hut he drew a 'Lakshman Rekha' with the tip of his arrow encircling the hut and told her not to go beyond it and if anyone who forcibly crossed the line would be burnt to ashes. As soon as Lakshman left, Ravan jumped at the opportunity. He took the form of the Saint and appeared in front of Sita's hut asking for alms. She stood behind the Lakshman Rekha while she was giving the alms but Ravan pretending to be a saint suddenly burst with anger and told her to step out of the line. As soon as she crossed the line Ravan revealed himself to her. He assured his original ten-headed demon form and loomed large before the scared Sita. Stunned by Ravan's act, she forgot to get back inside the circle and rebuked him saying my husband is most valiant man in the world and you are no match for his greatness so go back to Lanka! This made Ravan furious immediately seized her by the hand pulled her up to his flying chariot Pushpak Vimaan and flew towards Lanka. As Sita struggled to free herself screaming for help the King of Vultures, Jatayu heard her and went to her rescue but sadly the brave Jatayu was defeated by Ravan and he fell down to earth helpless.

On the way she saw group of monkeys sitting on the hill and she thought "I'll drop one of my garments here perhaps it may help My Lord and Lakshman to find me.

Ravan now flew nonstop to his own Kingdom of Lanka there he took Sita to Ashok vatika and placed her under an Ashok tree. Sita sat under the tree remembering Ram as she had seen him last running after the golden deer. She wept bitterly remembering Ram.

Ram returning to the forest hut was surprised to see Lakshman coming towards him. He said Lakshman what are you doing here? Why did you disobey me and leave Sita alone? Lakshman answered with tears in eyes, Mother Sita ordered me to go for your help as you were in danger without realising that the disguised voice belong to Marich, but she was very unsure about you and asked me to help you. By the time Ram and Lakshman realised that it was a trick Sita was already gone. They searched for her everywhere but could not find them. Ram called out Sita's name again and again but to no avail. He cried out Sita has been kidnapped O! Sita". Suddenly they came across the dying Jatayu who was lying nearby.

He said "Oh Lord ! Sita has been abducted by Ravan the ten-headed demon of Lanka; I have failed My Lord I tried to fight him but I failed" said Jatayu crying. He continued I was waiting to tell you this I cannot live more. By saying this Jatayu breath his last. Ram was moved to tears when he heard Jatayu's words, he embraced him and performed his last rites.

Ram meets Sugreev

Then Ram and Lakshman left Panchvati in search of Sita. On the way they met a cursed demon Kabandh. His body parts had been interchanged. His mouth was on his belly, his eyes on his chest. Ram and Lakshman freed him from the curse. Grateful, Kabandh asked them what had brought them to this mountain. Ram told him about Ravan and abduction of Sita. Hearing this Kabandh said to Ram "Ravan is extremely powerful, and you will not be able to fight him alone. You need a powerful ally go to the Rishimukha mountain and find Sugreev both of you can help each other". Ram and Lakshman thanked Kabandh and made their way towards Rishimukha mountains. While crossing the jungle Ram and Lakshman reached the simple abode of Shabari. Shabari was a staunch devotee of Ram when she saw Ram and Lakshmanshe said "You've come my Lord!Sage Matanga had assured me I would meet you my Lord before I die". Delighted at the visit, Shabari washed their feet with cold water and gave them a comfortable seat. She gathered fruits and bulbs from the forest and offered them to Ram and Lakshman then she sat devotedly in front of Ram.

Ram assured Shabari that she was amongst the greatest devotees. Then Ram and Lakshman bid goodbye to Shabari. Before leaving Shabari asked why they were roaming in the forest. Ram then narrated the whole incident of Sita abduction. Then later Shabari guided them the direction towards Rishimukha mountain. Ram and Lakshman made their way towards the mountain. From his hidden abode upon the hills Sugreev saw two brothers approaching. He told Hanuman his minister "Lok at those two young men coming in this direction it is not often that strangers wandered in the monkey kingdom." Hanuman said "They look very purposeful and strong I'll find out who they are". Sugreev said "But take care go disguised as brahmin and make enquiry. You must checkout their intentions and inform me by a sign. For if they've been sent by the wild Bali, I must leave this island flea at once".

Hanuman at once disguised himself and ran downhill and bowed respectfully to the visitors. He asked them "Who are you two heroes one dark and other fair? Why are you roaming in the forest in the guise of kshatriyas?". Ram replied we are the sons of Dashrath, the King of Kosala. We are in the forest to obey our father's command. My name is Ram and this is my brother Lakshman and we had with us my pretty wife Sita. Ravan has carried away my Janaki. It is to search for her that we are wandering here."

When Hanuman recognised Ram, he fell to his feet. Ram lifted Hanuman to his feet and clasped him in warm embrace.

Hanuman, the son of wind God Vayu was thrilled and transformed into his original form. Ram then asked him "Where can I find Sugreev? Hanuman, the mighty son of wind then carried two brothers on both his shoulder and flew off the top of the Mountain where Sugreev sat waiting for him.

# Ram kills Bali

When Sugreev saw Hanuman flying to him with the two brave youths, he felt very happy. Sugreev received them with reverence. He said, "I am highly blessed by your presence". Ram and Lakshman embraced Sugreev warmly. It was then Hanuman told Sugreev that Ram and Lakshman were searching for Sita who had been taken away by Ravan. Sugreev then recalled the site he had witnessed some time ago. I was sitting with my ministers on that hill. I saw a pretty woman being carried away, weeping continuously".

She cried out for you and when she saw us, she threw a garment down. Ram was thrilled to hear some news of Sita. Sugreev handed him the garment.

Ram pressed the cloth to his bosom and was lost in her thought. Sugriva assured Ram that he will do all he can to bring back Sita. Ram thanked him at the night while they were all sitting together Ram asked Sugreev "Why do you stay in this forest?".

Sugreev narrated the story."I have a brother Bali. We were so close that there are no words to describe our brotherly bond. One day a demon named Mayavi came to our Kishkindha city. In the middle of the night, he challenged Bali by shouting at our city gate. Bali, who was our King decided to accept the challenge. I accompanied my brother not letting him go alone. The demon Mayavi ran into a deep cave in the mountains. My brother Bali chased him and went inside the cave. I was instructed by Bali that I must wait here for a fortnight if Bali does notreturn, we must accept that he have been slain."

I was forced to do that. I waited for a month at the mouth of the cave. Then one day I saw a huge stream of blood coming out from it. I thought that my poor brother must have been killed so I blocked the cave so that the demon could not come out. When I returned to the city without Bali the ministers insisted on grounding me the King of Kishkindha. But Bali was not dead, he killed the demon and returned to the palace. Bali was very furious and gave me a sound beating. He took away the throne and the crown and even separated me from my beloved wife. It is out of fear of Bali that I am forced to live in the forest in hiding". Ram asked him that why don't he follow you hear too. The fear of Bali had driven him to seek shelter under Rishimukha mountain. Bali would not come fearing the curse of sage Matanga.

Ram was moved to hear Sugreev's plight and pledged to help him. He told Sugreev "Listen Sugreev, I'll slay Bali with a single arrow even if he tries to get the help of God's he won't escape".

At that very moment Jambvand, the divine King of Bears created by Lord brahma arrived. Everyone greeted him. He told Ram that Bali is very strong! Come I will show you the proof of his valour.

Jambvand led everyone to the forest he showed Ram and Lakshman the remains of the demon Dundubhi that Bali killed and threw here. He also showed Ram row of seven palm trees and said whosoever brings down this tree in one arrow is mighty to beat Bali. With a single well-aimed arrow Ram brought down all the seven trees. Sugreev was convinced of Rams prowess and felt his troubles were over. Thus, assured of Ram support Sugreev went to Bali to challenge him for a fight. Bali was surprised to hear Sugreev calling so bravely he ran out to confront him. His wife Tara cautioned him not to take the challenge, but he ignored her advice. Ram stood away behind the tree in the dense forest. Sugreev challenged Bali into a dual fight. The two brothers began fighting fiercely in the dense forest where Ram stood ready to kill Bali. But Ram was bewildered, he failed to differentiate Bali from Sugreev the two brothers were so similar in form, features and methods of fighting. Ram feared that he might kill Sugreev by mistake. Thus, at the end Sugreev fled for life to Rishimukha mountain.

Sugreev angrily asked Ram "Why didn't you kill Bali? I was about to die today". Ram then told him the reason that you brothers looked so similar that I was confused which one was Bali. So, I adviseyou to wear a Garland around your neck so that I would be able to identify him. Sugreev was satisfied and his spirits were recovered.

As the evening approached, he once again roared at the gates of Kishkindha. The two brothers pounced on each other. They were fighting constantly. Sugreev's body fled from several injuries. Seeing Sugreev unable to fight anymore Ram picked up his bow and shot an arrow at Bali from behind the tree.

But even as he tried his last breath, he raised his eyes to Ram as he recognised the Lord. He asked

RAMAYAN - An Epic Tale

Ram, "Why am I your foe and Sugreev your friend why Ram why?

Rams heart was filled with sorrow, but he spoke harsh words. Ram said "Listen you wretch! A younger brother's wife, a sister, a daughter in law and one's own daughter are alike whoever cast an evil eye on any of the four can be killed without any sin".

Bali realised his mistake and made a request "My son Angad is strong like me! Take him under your wing and accept him". Thus, assured Bali gasped his last breath. His death brought all his subjects together to limit the loss of their leader. Bali's wife Tara was inconsolable she cried helplessly. Sugreev then performed the last rites of his brother with due ceremony.

Then Ram asked Lakshman "Go to Kishkindha and arrange for a coronation of Sugreev". Owing to his woes of staying in the forest for 14 years of his exile Ram couldn't enter the city. Sugreev was crowned as a king and Angad was made the Crown Prince. Sugreev then immediately set to work. His first task was to help Ram find Sita.

➢ **'परहित सरिस धर्म नहीं भाई, परपीड़ा सम नहीं अधमाई'**

There is nothing more pious than doing good to others.

And there is nothing more wicked than causing harm to others!!

➢ **पद कमल धोइ चढ़ाइ नाव न नाथ उतराई चहौं।**
मोहि राम राउरि आन दसरथसपथ सब साची कहौं॥
बरु तीर मारहुँ लखनु पै जब लगि न पाय पखारिहौं।
तब लगि न तुलसीदास नाथ कृपाल पारु उतारिहौं॥

"I would like to wash the lotus-feet of yours. I do not expect any payment O Ram! I swear by your name and the name of Dasharath, I will get you across the river in my boat only after washing your feet."

➢ **राम ब्रह्म ब्यापक जग जाना, परमानंद परेस पुराना**

Ram is the all-pervading Ravan. He is the supreme bliss,

The highest lord and the most ancient being, as is known to the whole world!!

In search of Sita

Sugreev had all the monkeys from all the corners of the world to assemble before him. Sugreev gave orders to his huge army that Sita must be found within a month. Before Hanuman set out, he went to Ram to take his blessings. Ram embraced Hanuman. He took out a signet ring with Ram engraved on it and said "Take the ring and give it to Sita when you meet her, I have complete faith that you shall find my Sita, Hanuman!!"

The monkeys and the bear spread in all direction Hanuman, Angad and Jambvand and few more monkeys travel towards South. They had carefully searched forest, mountains, rivers and cities. In the days of search, they once reached a dense forest. They reached a strange place, and saw a resplendent garden with the lake covered with pretty lotuses. In a magnificent temple, sat a woman engrossed in prayer. From a respectful distance, Hanuman explained her their mission. They washed at the lake and ate the refreshments lovingly offered by the woman. She said, "Now all of you must close your eyes and go out of this temple. You will succeed to your search for Sita". They did it as told and when everyone opened their eyes instead of being in the middle of the dense forest, they found themselves standing on the seashore. They were all wondering a month is almost over how can we return without any news.

They met and old vulture named Sampatti who made use of his keen eyesight and told the monkeys that Sita was being held captive by Ravan in his kingdom Lanka which was located across the ocean. But before that, Sampatti was going to kill all the monkeys then Hanuman remembered that Sampatti was the elder brother of Jatayu. Hanuman saidthat Jatayu tried to prevent Ravan from taking Sita away but lost his life. Sampatti was pained to hear the news of his brother's demise and requested them to carry him to the sea to perform the last rites of Jatayu.

Hanuman asked him about his wings. Sampatti narrated the story "Once we were young, Jatayu and I tried to fly towards the sun. Jatayu was going to give up, but I went above high and high. However soon my wings were scratched by the suns ray, and I fell to the earth with a fearful scream. I fell near the feet of the Sage Chandram. He was kind to me and taught me how to get rid of my foolish pride". So, after helping the monkeys, Sampatti retired.

Now all the monkeys were strong and brave, but none could leap across the mighty ocean. Jambvand turned to Hanuman "You are brave strong and swift like your father the wind God, You are veritable storehouse of intelligence, discretion, and knowledge". Hanuman was encouraged by their praise and began to grow, soon as he was tall as a mountain, he ordered all the monkeys to wait for his return. Hanuman had been reminded by his powers by Jambvand which he often forgot because of the curse on him when he was a child.

Hanuman begins his journey

Hanuman started his journey by saying "Victory to Ram", seeing this noble act the Gods and all other heavenly creatures rained flowers on him. The Gods although pleased with his dedication to Lord Ram decided to further test his wisdom. So, they called upon Surasa, the Mother of the Serpents to place an obstacle in his way. Down their Hanuman flew on and on across the skies over the sea. Suddenly, Surasa stopped him by blocking his path. Surasa took the form of a hideous monster and charged at Hanuman. She told him "I have been given a boon no one can get past me you have to enter my mouth".

Hanuman did not have time to fight demons, so he was quick to outsmart her. He quickly shrank, swiftly flew into her mouth and immediately flew back out even Surasa was surprised at his quick wit; she was indeed pleased with him. Turning into her original form she blessed him and allowed him to continue his journey. Hanuman joyfully resumed his journey through the skies, but his troubles were not getting over in the depth of the sea there dwelt a deadly demoness. Seeing a reflection of flying creatures on the sea water she could grab their shadows and suspend their flight. When she saw Hanuman, she was thrilled at the mighty treat she would have done same with him, but Hanuman saw through her trickery and escaped unscratched. At last, he reached across the stretch of the sea.

RAMAYAN - An Epic Tale

Hanuman meets Sita

It was a wonderful forest with a very high golden walls and enclosed by the ocean on all sides. Hanuman saw a mighty army guarding the city on all the sides. Hanuman thought to himself "I can't get passed this gigantic guards I must become so tiny that they can't notice me then I can slip into the city". He assumed a form as small as a mosquito and entered Lanka, he then assumed his original form, but it was then that demoness Lankini saw him. She was the resident demon of the doorway of Lanka. He defeated her as well. Hanuman again assumed his tiny form to explore the city. A little ahead Hanuman saw a small palace which attracted his attention. the magnificent mansion had a small temple and a tulsi plant in the courtyard. There he met Vibhishana and narrated his story. Vibhishana then told Hanuman about Sita he told "She sits under a big tree in the lovely Ashok vatika surrounded by demoness". Hanuman again turned into a tiny mosquito form and flew to the Ashoka tree grove.

Soon as he hovered over it at the centre of Ashoka Garden, he saw a beautiful but sad looking woman. He immediately knew that it was Sita. Hanuman hid himself in the tree leaves when he heard a moment.

Soon Ravan arrived with the number of beautiful, bedecked damsels. Ravan tried to convince Sita in different ways cajoling, threatening, pleading to become his queen.

He said to her "O! fair faced one! all this Queens including Mandodri will become your hand maidens if you consent to marry me". Having plucked a blade of grass Sita spoke "Ravan all your powers are like this blade to me. I think you to be cowardly thief, if you wish to live seek forgiveness at the feet of Lord Ram".

Ravan returned sad and disheartened. Hanuman was very sad at this sight. Then as soon as Ravan went a demoness came and she was telling something politely to Sita. Hanuman was surprised, he waited for all the demoness to sleep so that he could meet Mother Sita. When the night fell, the demoness went to sleep. Hanuman started singing songs of Ram's birth till the end. Sita was delighted to hear it. She asked the singer to come before her. Hanuman did as he was told, he appeared before Sita and told her "Mother I am Hanuman, messenger of Lord Ram. He gave me this ring to give it to you. Do not grieve anymore, very soon Lord Ram and Lakshman would attack Lanka, Ravan and his army would be defeated and Lord Ram will carry you safely back home".

Sita was delighted and her heart was filled with joy and hope. Hanuman then narrated the event that led Ram and Lakshman to make friends with monkey King Sugreev and his army. Sita was convinced by the story. She told Hanuman "Please ask my lord to come early because Ravan has given me time of one month or else, he'll kill me". Hanuman agreed.

Hanuman's work was over, and he realised he was famished after his long flight. Sita said, "Go ahead but there are demons guarding all doors". Hanuman attacked the guards and began to eat the fruits. He killed some of the guards and others ran away in fear to Ravan's palace. Ravan sent some strong soldiers to confront Hanuman, but they were no match for him. Ravan then sent his son Akshay.

Hanuman killed him too, seeing the dead body of his brother, Indrajeet was filled with rage and went to fight Hanuman but he was instructed by Ravan to capture him and not kill him. He agreed to do so.

RAMAYAN - An Epic Tale

Meanwhile, Mandodri was devastated on hearing the news that is favourite son was killed. Indrajeet used brahmastra on Hanuman, an invisible weapon given to him by Lord brahma. When Hanuman realised that he was stuck by brahmastra he surrendered out of respect for Lord brahma. Indrajeet quickly bound him with ropes and represented him to Ravan in his court. The whole court was brilliant and dazzling with gold, gems, pearls, and silk. Hanuman stood tall and fearless before Ravan.

Ravan asked him "Who are you monkey? On whose might did you dare to destroy my orchards?Haven't you heard of my might?

Hanuman advised Ravan to beg Ram's forgiveness, but his advice enraged the demon king. Ravan wanted Hanuman to be killed, but it was his brother Vibhishana who was wiseadvised Ravan that it is not ethical to kill the messenger. Ravan agreed and said "He must be punished in some way; Monkey's tail is the most prized part of his body. Set his tail on fire and let him go".

Ravan's demon servant at once took Hanuman out, they wrapped his tail in racks. While Hanuman kept on elongating his tail and the demons kept on wrapping it. Soon after, not a single piece of cloth was left in Lanka. Everyone mocked at Hanuman. When Sita in Ashoka garden heard about Hanuman plight, she kindled a fire and prayed to the fire God, "Oh! Agni if I'm virtuous and pure at heart, Please be cool to my son Hanuman and do not hurt him in anyway." As soon as they set fire on his tail, Hanuman slipped out. Then he jumped with his blazing tail till the top of the tall building and reduced it to ashes springing from places to places. He assumed is gigantic form and soon set the entire city on fire. In the entire Kingdom only one palace was untouched by the fire which was Vibhishana'spalace.

Before going back, he went to meet Sita. Sita was overwhelmed and gave her chudamani (an ornament wore in hair) to Hanuman as a token of love for Lord Ram. She gave her blessings to Hanuman. Then he resumed his journey of going back to seashore where the monkeys were waiting for him. They were all shouting, He has come!!!Our saviour has come back from Lanka.

   RAMAYAN - An Epic Tale

Ram to build a bridge

Hanuman along with Vanar Sena headed back to meet their King Sugreev, Lord Ram and Lakshman. They were all overjoyed when they returned. Hanuman then narrated what had happened and handed out Sita's jewel chudamani to Ram. He clasped the chudamani to his heart. Everyone was sad when they heard of Sita's plight. Hanuman also told Ram and Lakshman that they had only one month's time to attack Lanka.

Ram said to Sugreev "Hanuman has performed a miracle. He has preserved Sita's life by consoling her. He has also saved my life by bringing good news about Sita."

At the head of the enormous horde was Ram strong and brave leading his army to the victory of good over evil. The mighty army reached the seashore and rested. The main question was how will the huge armycross the seashore? Ram sat down near the shore and offered prayers to the Ocean God.

But his prayers fell flat on the deaf ears of the Ocean God. Ram was now full of rage and asked Lakshman to bring his bow and arrow he got ready to dry up the ocean. Seeing what Ram was about to do, Ocean God got scared and appeared immediately "O! Ram it is my nature that no one can cross me, but you can take help of Nal and Neel the sons of God of Architecture, Vishwakarma. They can build a bridge across me all I can do is to help it to assure you that my sea creatures shall not harm and attack you or your army".

Ram ordered Nal and Neel to start the construction of bridge. All the monkeys begin that search of big tree trunks and big rocks. Meanwhile in Lanka the news of the enemy's approachreached Lanka.

Ravan's wife Mandodri was disturbed, Vibhishana pleaded Ravan to seek Ram's forgiveness and free Sita but in vain. Ravan kicked him, this made Vibhishana to join Rams army who happily welcomed him. Meanwhile Ram built a Shivalinga and was praying to Lord Shiva. The Shivalinga made by Ram is today known as Rameswaram.

The construction of bridge was going very rapidly fast, on each rock Hanuman used to write 'Ram' and then give it to Nal and Neel to float in the water. The bridge was ready and the whole army marched onto the bridge and reached Lanka. They camped out in Lanka for that night.

Angad as a peace messenger

While they were all sitting, Vibhishana explained them how the gates were protected, how to get pass them and more details about Lanka. Ram decided to send Angad as a messenger of peace to Ravan the next morning. As the sun rose, Angad took blessings of Lord Ram, and all the elders present and he set out to Ravan's court. Angad entered Ravan's court and stood there tall and unfeared. He told Ravan "I am a messenger of Lord Ram. My father and you used to be friends. I used to respect you but having carried Mother Sita, You are a coward to me. If you don't want to be killed, seek forgiveness of Lord Ram and return Mother Sita".

Ravan laughed heartily and told "So now Ram is scared of me and he is sending you all the monkeys here instead of fighting with me". He was insulting Lord Ram. Seeing this Angad was filled with fury and said "I have placed my foot in the middle of the court. If your warriors are that brave, ask them to move my foot and if they succeed in doing that, I, on behalf of Lord Ram will accept defeat and will go back from Lanka". Ravan urged all his champions to move Angad's foot but despite of their efforts they could not even move it. At last Ravan rose to try his might. When Ravan came, Angad moved his foot and said, "You fool don't touch my foot. Touch the feet of Lord Ram and your life will be saved". Angad went back and narrated what all had happened.

Ravan soon declared war!!

Having got the news about war, Ram called out a meeting with his chiefs.

The epic battle begins

That night Meghnath ordered all his soldiers to attack the camps of Ram while they were all unaware about the attack. A few monkeys got killed. Hearing the sounds, everyone came out and soon they realised that they had been attacked from the enemy. Meghnath became invisible and began to fire the tents. Ram could sense him and shot deadly arrows at him but missed. Meghnath decided to

RAMAYAN - An Epic Tale

shoot serpent arrow at Ram and Lakshman and was succeeded in doing so.

Hanuman, Sugreev, Jambvand, Angad all were very worried. Ram and Lakshman's body started to become blue and black. Meanwhile in Lanka, Ravan and his family were celebrating their victory. Sita was devastated to hear the news and demanded an answer from Lord Shiva.

Lord Shiva sent Pakshiraj Garuda to revive Lord Ram and Lakshman. Pakshiraj licked their feet, and soon a miracle happened and they slowly started to gain consciousness. They both thanked Garuda Dev.

Next day in the battlefield Ravan sent Dhumraksh who was very tall and poisonous, but Ram easily defeated Dhumraksh.

Ravan and Meghnath were devastated due to Ram's victory. But Ravan still did not accept his defeat and summoned Akampana and their whole group. Next day, in the battlefield Ravan send some of the commander in chiefs along with Akampana's whole army. Ram didn't need to fight that day.

His warriors were capable of fighting, Lakshman attacked Akampana but as per Ram's order did not kill. Everyone was captured. They were all very unhappy and shared their grief with Ram that they wanted freedom and were pressurized by Ravan. Ram assured them that they will have the freedom to be free.

Ravan was very angry when he heard this.

Meanwhile in the tent, Vibhishana instructed everyone about the powerful asuras that Ravan had summoned to fight against them.

First was Devantak, who was very powerful enough and with the help of his horns, it made easier for him to fight.

Second was Vajramushti, whose body was made of coal. His body was so strong that no weapon could be used against him.

Third was Supaksh, who's half body was snake and half asura. With the help of his poison, he could kill many people at a time.

RAMAYAN - An Epic Tale

That night Supaksh attacked their camps using his poison and one by one all the monkey's fell unconscious. Nal, Neel, Sugreev one by one all fell unconscious. Ram, Lakshman, Hanuman and Vibhishana were all very worried. Due to Sita's akhand jyot they were all alive yet. To make them all alive again Ram prayed to Lord Shiva and made a shivling. Lord Shiva healed the Vanar Sena. Ram thanked Lord Shiva and took his blessings.

Ram challenged Ravan to fight with him face to face and not attack his army again and again like a coward. While the Vanar senawas trying to get in the palace. The Vanar Sena made an attemptto enter Ravan's fort from all sides but due to some difficulties, they were not able to enter. Meanwhile, Ravan asked Vajramushti to fight Ram.

The next day, Vajramushti entered the battlefield and stood there tall and unharmed. He tried to scare the Vanar sena but defeated in doing so. Hanuman offered Ram to lift him so that he can be of Vajramushti's height. Vajramushti told Ram "It would be an insult for Ravan to fight with you". Vibhishana had warned Ram earlier that it was not easy to win against Vajramushti. So, remembering that, Ram carefully observed him and then aimed his arrow on his neck and his whole body was burnt to ashes, and he died soon after. Vibhishana asked him "How did you kill Vajramushti so easily? Ram told him that "I knew that his neck was the most weak part of his body." Everyone hailed Lord Ram.

Ravan was very angry on hearing Vajramushti's death. With the help of his secret messenger Vibhishana got to know that Ravan was going to come in the battlefield the following day. Meghnath and his mother Kaikasi tried to convince Ravan to not go to the battlefield because he had so many powerful warriors still left but he paid no heed to their advice. Ram and Ravan came face to face the next day. But before fighting Ravan wanted to ask Ram a few questions. Ravan questioned him "Why did you cut Shurpanakha's nose"? Ram answered that "I believe that what happened that day was not true, if you wanted to take revenge you should have fought with me, why did you abduct Sita"? Lakshman got angry on seeing Ram talking with Ravan.

Ravan said that "Sita's biggest mistake was being your wife". Ram responded to him by talking about the true nature of knowledge. When Sita got to know about Ravan and Ram's encounter, she became worried and started chanting prayers, even Trijata accompanied her in doing so.

Ravan asked Ram to fight. Ram saw that the sun was setting and didn't want to fight and told him that "It is a 'Dharmayudha' and we should follow the rules".

Ravan returned to his palace angrily. Meghnath and Kaikasi questioned Ravan "How is Ram alive till now?" Why didn't you kill him?

Ravan decided to meet Sita in Ram's disguise so that he could easily trick her. Meanwhile Hanuman told Sugreev and Angad that destroying Ravan's ego is more important than defeating him in the battle. Even Lakshman was very angry, but Ram explained him.

Ravan decided to turn himself as Ram in disguise. Mandodri tried to explain himbut in vain. With the help of some sources Ravan succeeded in taking

Ram's disguise. Later Ravan entered his court in Ram's disguise and was getting prepared to meet Sita. Soon after, he went to meet Sita in the Ashok Vatika. When he entered the Ashok vatika, Sita ran to meet him. Then Ravan spoke "I have come to vanish all your sorrows, in this separation we had to face many hardships for each other." At that very moment Sita thought that something was not right. He continued bragging about himself and said the King of Lanka has kept you here in this Nirjan vatika?

Even Sita started insulting more and more about Ravan and got a clue that it was Ravan in Ram's disguise. Ravan at last showed his original form and was very angry now as his plan failed yet again.

RAMAYAN - An Epic Tale

Kumbhkaran meets his end

Ravan returned to his palace furious and fuming. Ravan thinks for a moment to free Sita. He is supported by Mandodri, but he remains the same old Ravan.

Meanwhile Vibhishana worshiped Lord Vishnu in his tent, Ram seeing this tells that there is so much difference between you and Ravan. Vibhishana told him that there was a time when Ravan was also the same, they used to share a great bond. But because of Ravan's bad deeds, everything changed. Ram responded that "It is always very difficult to be on the good side". Meanwhile in Ravan's court he was preparing to go in the battlefield the next day but Mandodri's father Mayasura stopped him. Ravan was surprised to see him but he told Ravan that "You are my daughter's husband and it is my duty to help you in your time of need". Meghnath asked whether he can go in the battle but Mayasura denied and told him that he is the Yuvraj, the future king and thus cannot go. Ravan wasbaffled that who will go to the battlefield? Mayasura said that someone huge and big will go and asks them to think who it is?

   RAMAYAN - An Epic Tale

Ravan told "My brother Mahabali Kumbhkaran will fight tomorrow". Meanwhile arrangements were made to awake Kumbhkaran. With great difficulty Ravan made Kumbhkaran awake from his sleep. In Lanka Ravan narrated the whole story to Kumbhkaran, once he was awake. Sita got to know about Kumbhkaran, then she suddenly remembered Lakshman who didn't sleep for fourteen years for his brother. Trijata told her that even Kumbhkaran is like Vibhishana and is a 'Dharmatma'.

Kumbhkaran warned Ravan that "Ram is not a common man he appears to be divine so it will be our own good if we don't fight with him." Ravan on hearing this argues with him. Kumbhkaran tried to make Ravan understand his mistake but in vain. He said Ravan that "You did not do the right thing by abducting Sita". But agrees to fight with him for Ravan.

Kumbhkaran also warned him that "If Idon't return tomorrow and get killed by Ram, assume that he is not an ordinary man. No one can defeat him. Meanwhile Vibhishana got the news that Kumbhkaran was going to come in the battlefield. He told Ram that "Kumbhkaran is mymost beloved brother". He continued that Kumbhkaran has not done bad deeds in his whole life.

Ram said that he has only taken this decision to follow his elder brother's command. He tells everyone to be prepared for tomorrow. Vibhishana is devastated as he knows that his brother will be killed tomorrow.

Mandodri asked his father "Why did you support Ravan? You know what he is doing is not at all right." Her father responded "We can't stop him now. We have reached a stage in the war that either Ram or Ravan is going to be destroyed. I had no other option but to support him". Before going in the battlefield, Kumbhkaran takes his mother's blessings. Kaikasi said that "I am very proud to have a son like you andvery happy that you are going to fight for Ravan". She gave Kumbhkaran blessings that he will win, but Kumbhkaran stopped her. He told her that if she wants to give him blessings that in the battlefield, he will be firm in his decision. Kaikasi was shocked to hear this. Meanwhile Trijata told Sita that Kumbhkaran was going to fight today. In the tent Ram made a strategy to fight Kumbhkaran.

Vibhishana was very worried for his brother and was consoledby Ram. Kumbhkaran tried to scare away the Vanar sena. Vibhishana told Lakshman and Hanuman how food was arranged for him and the boon granted to him. Sugreev challenged Kumbhkaran but he told Sugreev that he wanted to fight Ram and not all the monkeys. Lakshmana asked Ram whether he can fight Kumbhkaran, but Vibhishana toldhim that he wanted to try to convince Kumbhkaran not to fight.

Vibhishana came in front of Kumbhkaran and he tried topersuade Kumbhkaran not to fight against Ram, but Kumbhkaran told him that it was his duty to follow his brother's command. Kumbhkaran told him that he will be known as "Lanka bhedi Vibhishana". Later Kumbhkaran challenged Ram into a duel.

Hanuman stopped Kumbhkaran when he tried to crush Angad under his foot. Lakshman told Kumbhkaran to get past him before fighting Ram. Meanwhile Sita was very worried for Ram,

Lakshman and the Vanar sena. Kumbhkaran removed his weapons and Lakshman one by one crushed them with no difficulty. He told Lakshman that "You are also no ordinary man; you slay all my powerful weapons in one go." Kumbhkaran then took out his trishul. Vibhishana told Ram that "That this is a Shiva's identical trishul and no weapon can stop this trishul". Ram panicked.

Kumbhkaran throwed the trishul at Lakshman. Hanuman stopped the trishul and saved Lakshman.

Vibhishana told Ram "Kumbhkaran's anger is very dangerous". Later Kumbhkaran found out that Ram was an incarnation of Lord Vishnu andthat he had taken an avatar to release me and brother Ravan. Mother Sita in the Ashok vatika was none other than Jag Janani Mata Lakshmi. But then he thought that if he went to him, Ram will forgive him and he will not get released. So, he challenged Ram. He told Kumbhkaran "You have done nothing wrong so I can't fight with you. So please go back to Lanka, and don't be a part of Ravan's misdeeds". Kumbhkaran thought to himself that "My life should end in the hands of Lord Ramonly or else

                    RAMAYAN - An Epic Tale

I will not be released". So, he attacked Ram. He cut of his both hands and legs.

Kumbhkaran told him that "It is my misfortune that I am not able to bow you as I have no hands, but I feel myself very lucky to die in the hands of you." Saying this he died.

Ram needs Ravan

Meanwhile, Ravan got the news that Kumbhkaran is killed. He was furious and was not ready to believe what had happened. Meghnath tried to console him but Ravan was outraged on him as well as Kaikasi. Kumbhkaran cannot be killed, he can only be killed by Vishnu. How can he be killed by a Vanar? Even Mayasura tried to console him. Ravan in anger decided to kill Sita and blamed her for everything that happened. Mayasura stopped him. He told nothing can stop me from killing Sita. Kaikasi remembered the last words of Kumbhkaran and cried very much, this made Ravan change his mind of not killing Sita. Kaikasicouldn't believe that out of the three sons only one was left.

Later Mandodri consoles her, Kaikasi realises her mistakes and orders to stop the war. Ravan became furious on hearing this and blames Mandodri for this. Kaikasi made Ravan understand that it is good if you realise your mistakes in time being you should mend it but Ravan laughs and does not try to understand. When Kaikasi decides to send a messenger to Ram, Ravan kills him.

Meanwhile Ram Lakshman wishes to perform a ritual on Dashrath's death anniversary and tells Hanuman and Sugreev.

Sugreev praises him, Lakshman tells him that there is no brahmin in the region and we need vedapatti. Vibhishana arrives there at that moment and tells that Ravan killed all the brahmins in the Kingdom. Jambvand suggest that why don't Vibhishana does the 'Darpan'. Vibhishana tells that he is not a vedapatti brahman. He tells that only one person can do this in whole Lanka Ram ask who?

Vibhishana tells that he will not do that darpan Lakshman says that we will plead ourselves. Vibhishana tells that he is none other than king Ravan later Hanuman says that he will convince Ravan and ask them to make preparation for the Darpan. Hanuman goes to the palace later Hanuman praises Ravan and request him to perform the rituals, Ravan is in a dilemma meanwhile Sita makes Kheer for Shradh.

Ravan goes for darpan next day, Ravan performs the rituals of Dasharatha's death anniversary, Ram asked for dakshina and Ravan used this opportunity and asked to give Sita to which Ram replied that guru dakshina can be given when we have that thing during pooja he said that he does not have Sita now and hence he cannot give it to him. He gives a part of holy water as guru dakshina Ravan returns to his palace dejected meanwhile Ravan's father Vishrava arrives at his palace Ravan takes the water to Ashok vatika and breaks it in front of Sita.

Ram kills Tarini

Vishrava tells Ravan that the two brothers in the battlefield are no ordinary man, Ram is no other than the Lord Hari Vishnu. He said that he cannot see the destruction of Lanka, but Ravan tells him that he's not scared of Vishnu. Kaikasi adds up that Kumbhkaran could only be killed by Vishnu, but Ravan ignores all this, but it's convinced to check whether it's true. Ravan decides to use Tarini to find out if Ram is really in avatar of Lord Vishnu after Vishrava informed him about the same. Mandodri is very worried on hearing this. Tarini leaved in a dark cave after his father had banished him from the palace due to his devotion for Lord Vishnu. Tarini was pleased to meet Ravan.

Ravan tells him about the war and tell him that if he succeeds, he can do Vishnu bhakti freely in the palace and he will also build a temple for him. Meanwhile in the tent Vibhishana tells Ram about Tarini's devotion towards Lord Narayan. Ravan prepares Tarini for the war, Kaikasi ask Vishrava for help to protect Ravan.

Kaikasi decides to build Sahastra Ravan who can protect Ravan. Vishrava refuses but Kaikasi convinces him that we must do this to protect her son. Tarini attacks the Vanar sena and challenges Ram to fight with him. Tarini sees Lord Vishnu in Ram before Ram kills him. Ravan gets the news of Tarini's death. Ravan questions lord brahma about sending Lord Vishnu to kill him in Ram's Avtar. He then remembered the boon Lord brahma had given to him that no one except human can kill Ravan.

Lakshman is critical

A boastful Ravan declares war against Lord Vishnu. Meghnath asks Ravan to give him permission to kill Ram and Lakshman and finish of their army. Meanwhile Trijata makes sculpture of Lord Ram. Vibhishana tells Lakshman that Meghnath is going to come today for war Lakshman is happy on hearing this. Vibhishana tells that we must be very careful from Meghnath, and he will come from the fifth door and the secret door of Lanka. Lakshman sets off to fight Meghnath without Rams permission Lakshman gets into a fierce combat with Meghnath Lakshman crashes down his chariot in the camp Ram is worried about Lakshman. Vibhishana tells him that Lakshman has gone to fight with Meghnath alone and Meghnath has taken him away from the battlefield Ram tells that without his permission Lakshman went to fight alone this has never happened before. Sugreev pacifies him to search Lakshman. Hanuman and Vanar Sena set out in search of him meanwhile Sita senses something bad, Lakshmanan Meghnath continue fighting. Meghnath uses his special powers and injures Lakshman who gets unconscious. Meanwhile Hanuman looks for Lakshman by flying he finds him laying down unconscious in the mud he carries him on his shoulder back to Ram.

Ram is shocked to see Lakshman in this state he calls out for Lakshman but receives no response. Ravan is happy that Meghnath killed Lakshman, he lies to Sita about Lakshman. They call out for a physician he tells Ram that it is life threatening case for Lakshman. He applies an ointment on the wound, but it takes no effect. Trijata tells Sita that Lakshman is critical the news is true. Sita is unable to believe and whips.

Ved tells Ram that Lakshman is critical Vibhishana tells that even he does not know about Meghnath powers. Trijata informs Sita about Meghnath's power which he first uses on himself and then Ved Sushen who lives in Lanka cures him. Sita tells Trijata to go and inform Ram about this.

Trijata tells Ram that only Sushen can save Lakshman Hanuman sets out to findSushen. Hanuman finds

Sushen'sashram and enters but finds no one and starts to leave but then he hears a noise and finds secret door in the ashram. He finds Sushen there. Sushen says that he has to live in this secret palace because of Meghnath. Hanuman asked Sushen to come with him to cure Lakshman. Sushen refuses but convinces him to do. Hanuman arrives with Sushen in the camp Ram greets him and request him to cure Lakshman. Sushen says that he must obey his king Ravan and support him Ram later tells him his duty as a Ved. He also assures Sushen that he's safe here no one can harm. Sushen tells Ram about the miraculous hub that can only cure Lakshman. He says that Sanjeevani booti can only be found in Himalayas. He tells that if Lakshman does not get Sanjeevani booti the till sunrise he will not be saved. It is nearly impossible to get Sanjeevani booti before sunrise.

Hanuman leaves for Himalayas in search of the herb when Meghnath gets the news that Sushen is not there in the ashram and a monkey has gone to Himalayas, he is very furious unable to believe it to stop Hanuman he sends asur in the form of a snake. Meanwhile Ram is very worried in the tent. Hanuman on the way meets a sage chanting Lord Rams name he told Hanuman that he knows the battle is going on and Lakshman was critical to impress Hanuman. Hanuman is pleased and asks the way to Himalaya. But when he assumes his real form, he traps Hanuman, but Hanuman kills him and tries to find his way to Himalaya. Hanuman reaches Himalaya but is unable to identify the Sanjeevani booti, so Hanuman takes the whole mountain with him later Ram is shocked to see Hanuman with the whole mountain Sushen takesSanjeevani booti and cures Lakshman.

Ram embraces Hanuman and thanks him. Lakshman is saved with Sanjeevani booti.

Sita is very happy on hearing the news later Ram makes a declaration that his brother Sumitra Nandan Lakshman will only kill Meghnath.

Meanwhile Sulochana has a bad dream that make Meghnath is killed by a Black Horse. She is very scared, and she sees that black horse everywhere Ravan confronts Meghnath for not killing Ram and Lakshman. Meghnath decides to worship Devi Nikumbhala to get the Ajay divine chariot.

Vibhishana tells Ram that they have to stop Meghnath from worshipping Devi Nikumbhala or else it would be impossible to kill Meghnath. Sulochana tries to stop him from going to puja and persuades it is not advisable because if the yagna gets spoiled before the conclusion the one who is doing it gets killed. She tells Mandodri even Mandodri tries to stop Meghnath but in vain. When he leaves for the yagna Lakshman, Hanuman, Sugreev, Neel and Nal and monkey troop set out to the Cave in which Meghnath was performing the yagna. They tried hard to break his meditation at last Hanuman puts water in the fire. Meghnath and Lakshman get into a fierce battle Sugreev tries to help Lakshman, but he refuses to do so. Lakshman kills Meghnath and tells Ram about it. Sulochana is heartbroken to see Meghnath body Ravan is furious to hear this. In anger and grief, Sulochana does not allow Ravan to touch Meghnaths body holding him responsible. She decidesto go to the battlefield to get Meghnaths head, Sita is scared that Lakshman will not give the head to Sulochana because he is very angry. She sends a letter to return the head to Sulochana and tells him that Sulochana is a religious lady Lakshman returns the head to Sulochana and apologises to her. Kaikasi and Vishrava starts to build Sahastra Ravan.

Next day indrajit's last rites were performed but Sulochanawas not present as she was getting ready and wanted to die in same flame with Meghnath. Mandodri stops her but in vain. Later Sita comes to the rescue and stops her, she pacifies her to take care of people he loved. Ravan performs last rites. Ram decides to crown Vibhishana as new king of Lanka after Ravan's death meanwhile Ahirravan promises Ravan that he will kill Ram and Lakshman.

Hanuman kills Ahirravan

Ahirravan attacks the camp one by one everybody falls unconscious Vibhishana is shocked to see Ram and his army lying unconscious. Ahirravan appears at that moment and takes ram and Lakshman to patal lok. He even makes Vibhishana unconscious. Hanuman is shocked that Ram and Lakshmanan are not there. one by one everybody wakes up Vibhishana tells Hanuman that Ahirravan has taken Ram and Lakshman to patal Lok.

Hanuman goes to patal lok to search for Ram and Lakshman while Sita gets the news that Ahirravan has taken and Ram Lakshman shefinds it hard to believe it. Devi Patalika decides not to accept any kind of sacrifice when Hanuman stops here from killing Ram and Lakshman. Impressed with Hanumans power she saysthat he will we also known as Patali Hanuman from now on.

Meanwhile Sita performs yogmaya in Ashok vatika, Hanuman kill Ahirravan, and while dying he asks Hanuman that how will he be able to wake Ram Lakshman.

Ram Lakshman wakes up because of yogmaya performed by Sita. Hanuman tells them the entire tale. Trijata tells Sita about Ram Lakshman arrival in Lanka. Hanuman brings Ram and Lakshman in the tents. Ram thanks Hanuman for saving their life Ravan tries to obtain all the powerful weapons Vishrava and Kaikasi continue making Sahastra Ravan. Ram prepares the strategy to fight, Vibhishana tells Ram about Ravan's weapon.

Ram and Ravan come face to face with each other Ram ask Nal and Neel to look after Vibhishana because he is Lanka's future king. Ram takes his bow and stringsit; the war begins Lakshman shoots an arrow at Supaksh. He sees that Lakshman is an avatar of Lord Vishnu's snake Sheshnaag and dies.

Ravan learns his secret

Ram destroys Ravan's chariot and one by one he uses all his weapons on Ravan but it takes no effect. As the sunset the war takes rest Ram is worried why Ravan remains unaffected in the face of the Vanar Sena's attack. Later Ravan ask Mandodri to prepare for medicine for his wounds Sita ask Trijata to deliver letter to Ram.

Ram feels happy on receiving Sita's letter. Vibhishana tells that it is not easy to defeat Ravan. Ram decides to perform shakti Aradhana and ask Hanuman to bring 108 lotuses. He can't find Lotus anywhere and decides to go to Sita, she helps him and gives him 108 lotuses meanwhile Ravan shocked to see that all the wounds have healed on their own. He asked Mandodri the reason, Mayasura tells him that his wife Mandodri went to chandralok and obtained amrut and placed it in his navel that is the reason behind the healing.

Ravan gets happy and is aesthetic that no one can kill him. He thanks Mandodri and ask if anyone else is aware of it. She says that Vibhishana only placed the Amrut in your navel. Ravan decides to kill Vibhishana on learning that he is aware of the Amrut kalash before he tells Ram. Mayasura and Mandodri tries to stop him but in vain. Ram is overjoyed to hear that Sita has given the Lotus as he begins the Shakti Aradhana. Lakshman informs that Ram will not get up until the puja is completed so he decides to stand there and ask everyone else to go to sleep but Hanuman insists on staying.

Ravan ask Shankini and Dankini to bring Vibhishana to him. They take disguise of Nal and Neel and puts Vibhishana's tent on fire and take him away.

Sugreev notices this and informs Hanuman that asuras have captured Vibhishana. Hanuman silently sneaks away without letting Ram know. Shankini and Dankini take Vibhishana to Ravan and ties him to a tree trunk. Ravan tries to kill Vibhishana, but Hanuman reaches at the moment and take the whole tree along with which Vibhishana was tied. They reach safely at the tent Vibhishana thanks Hanuman for saving him from Ravan. Ram continues to do his shakti Aradhana. He one by one offers Lotus to goddess Parvati. Parvati tells Shiva that if someone decides to do Shakti Aradhana then they have to give a test of the devotion and today even Ram is doing that Aradhana. Shiva tells her that she must do what is necessary Parvati vanishes one Lotus. When Ram notices that onelotus is missing, he thinks if he doesn't offer the last Lotus the Aradhana will remain incomplete. He remembers his mother Kausalya's word that he was having rajeevnayan meaning that his eyes were like lotus and decides to give them but at that very moment Ma Parvati arrives and stops him. Ram tells him that she has already accepted the Lotus and assures him that he will win against Ravan. Meanwhile Kaikasi and Vishrava continues the making of Sahastra Ravan Mandodri tries to tell Kaikasi to stop Ravan but in vain.

Ravan is dead

Next day Ram encourages the Vanar Sena. Vibhishana tells Ram that he cannot see the war today and decides to stay back in the tent. Ravan arrives in his Ajay Divya chariot and attacks the Vanar Sena using his elusive powers. Ram attacks Ravan, Hanuman offers to help Rambut he denies Ram manages to burn one part of his chariot later Trijata informs Sita about Ravan's attack on Vanar Sena. Indra gives his divine chariot

Ravan was angry on Indra because he gave his divine chariot to Ram. Ram manages to behead Ravan but is it all over? Ram gets off the divine chariot and Vanar Sena's celebrates their victory, but Ravan comes alive with his ten heads again.

Ram manages to cut Ravan's ten fearsome heads one more time but is shocked to see him come alive once again with his elusive powers Hanuman tries to find Vibhishana when Ravan remains unaffected. Meanwhile Ram and Ravan start wrestling, hearing the battle situation Vibhishana informs Ram that Ravan cannot dieas he has Amrit shakti stored in his umbilicus, the only way to kill him is to aim the arrow at the umbilicus and break the Amrit kalash.

As per the instructions Ram targets Ravan's umbilicus. Ravan hits the ground hard Vibhishana is devastated when he sees his brother in this state. Ravan could finally see Lord Vishnu's avatar in Ram and realises all his misdeeds during his last few moments of life. Ram ask Lakshman to take last minute knowledge from extremely learned person. Ravan breathes his last.

Vishrava tells Kaikasi about Ravan's death meanwhile Sita is extremely happy on hearing that Ravan's dead. Mandodri is full of tears and sorrow Vibhishana performs Ravan's last rites. Vishrava and Kaikasi performs a ritual to bring Sahastra Ravan to life.

Sahastra Ravan comes back to life

Sahastra Ravan comes back to life and attacks the tents. Ram and Lakshman are shocked. Vibhishana asks Ram to end Sahastra Ravan or else he will kill the whole world. Ram ask everyone to scatter in all four direction and attacks Sahastra Ravan everyone tries but fails finally Ram uses brahmastra against Sahastra Ravan but fails to kill him.

Sahastra Ravan attacks Ram and his army and makes them fall unconscious Parvati gets worried and ask Shiva to stop Sahastra Ravan.

Meanwhile Kaikasi tells Sita that Ram along with Vanar Sena is dead. Sita is shocked on seeing them unconscious later Sita takes up the form of Goddess Bhadrakali and kills Sahastra Ravan. When Ram wakes up, he thinks who killed Sahastra Ravan.

Ram announces Vanar Sena's victory over Lanka. Vibhishana stops Kaikasi from killing Sita who confronts him from deceiving the clan. Later Kaikasi breaks down and mourns the loss. Ram tells Vibhishana that he wants to meet Kaikasi.

Kaikasi goes to meet Ram along with Vibhishana. Kaikasi enquires Ram about his decision to crown the king of Lanka he tells Kaikasi that Vibhishana will be the king of Lanka. Later Ram appoints Vibhishana as the new king of Lanka.

Ram meets Sita

Lakshman goes to Ram and tells that we should go and meet Sita, but Ram tells him that he should first ask Sita's opinion and addresses her as "Devi". Lakshman is shocked on hearing this but follows his instruction. Sita is delighted on seeing Lakshman and eagerly waits for Ram. Trijata goes to prepare arti's thali for Ram. Sita is very jubilant on seeing Ram, but Ram addresses her as Devi and tells that he's sorry for all the hardships she has to go through and tells her that she was tide to him but today she can set herself free. Sita is shocked on hearing this, Ram tells her that she can't return to Ayodhyaand that she can live at any place of her choice Mithila, Lanka or any part of the world. Trijata hears this and tells everyone.

Everyone is awestruck on hearing this. Sita asks the reason behind the decision. Lakshman confronts Ram for his decision to abandon Sita. Shurpanakha arrives at that moment and tells "what will people think Sita has lived with Ravan will she be pure or not? Ram Lakshman Sita gets angry. Later Sita proves her fidelity to Ram by giving Agni pariksha she remembers her father's word that fire is very pure. She orders Lakshman to make arrangement for Agni pariksha she tells that if agnidev do not burn her it will be proved in the whole world that she is pure Lakshman refuses but is bound to follow. Ram tries to stop her but in vain Hanuman, Sulochana, Mandodri and everyone tries to stop her but she does not listen later she walks into the fire. Ram is dejected on seeing Sita walk into the fire, later Agnidev appears along with Sita and tells Ram that it is impossible for me to burn Sita because she is as much pure now till, she was before her abduction.

Ram was delighted on seeing Sita and hugs her. Later that evening Lakshman ask Ram the reason behind is decision. He tells Lakshman that he only wanted to protect Sita's purity in front of the world. Ram explains to Lakshman in detail, Lakshman apologises to Ram for being rude and angry. Hanuman arrives at the moment and says that he wants to tell something. He said when I was returning from Himalayas your brother Bharat stopped my way, he asked me all the

   RAMAYAN - An Epic Tale

questions where was I going etc when I said your name in the whole story he said "go fast but make sure you tell to Lord Ram that if they don't return after exact 14 years, they won't find me alive in Ayodhya".

Ram Sita Lakshman bid farewell to everyone in Lanka. Vibhishana advices Ram to take Ravan's pushpak vimana. Sugreev asked Angad to take the Vanar Sena to Kishkindha via the Setu route.

Ram Lakshman Sita in Ayodhya

Ram, Sita, Lakshman, Hanuman, Sugreev, Vibhishana, Jambvand altogether head to Ayodhya. Ram tells Sita that he wants to repent for all the sins during the war and decides to stop at Sage Bharadwaj ashram before reaching Ayodhya. Meanwhile Bharat prepares to kill himself as per his words to Ram. Kaushalya, Kaikeyi, Sumitra Mandavi Shatrughan tries to stop Bharat but in vain. Ram performs the darpan at the ashram and ask Hanuman to tell Bharat that they have reached in Ayodhya.

Bharat puts himself on fire but Hanuman doses the fire meanwhile Jambvand bids farewell to Ram. Hanuman tells Bharat about Ram Sita and Lakshman's arrival in Ayodhya.

Kaushalya, Kaikeyi and Sumitra are delighted to see them but when they arrive at Bharat's ashram. Ram clasp Bharat to his bosom. Bharat apologies Kaikeyi and hugs her. They all head to Ayodhya and are welcomed by the people. They take the blessings of Guru Vashistha Lakshman goes to wake up Urmila, Guru Vashistha asks Lakshman to worship Nidra Devi to wake up Urmila.

Urmila was delighted to see Lakshman later guru Vashistha fixes a date for Ram's coronation. Sugreev, Hanuman, Vibhishana makes arrangement for Ram's coronation. Ayodhya's citizen rejoices the grand day. Ram Sita get ready for the auspicious day. Guru Vashistha crowns Ram the king of Ayodhya all the people of Ayodhya were happy.

All of Ayodhya rejoiced and even the God in the heaven were delighted. Ram had achieved his aim and returned to rule Ayodhya and fulfil his father's wish

What followed afterwards was another chapter of struggle for Ram and Sita. This epic has been stated as "Uttar Ramayana".

Jai Shree Ram

> **बिनु सत्संग विवेक न होई, राम कृपा बिनु सुलभ न सोई**

The power to discriminate cannot be attained without keeping the company of saintly people.

And such company cannot be had without the grace of Shri Ram!!

जय श्री राम

King Dashratha's Family Tree

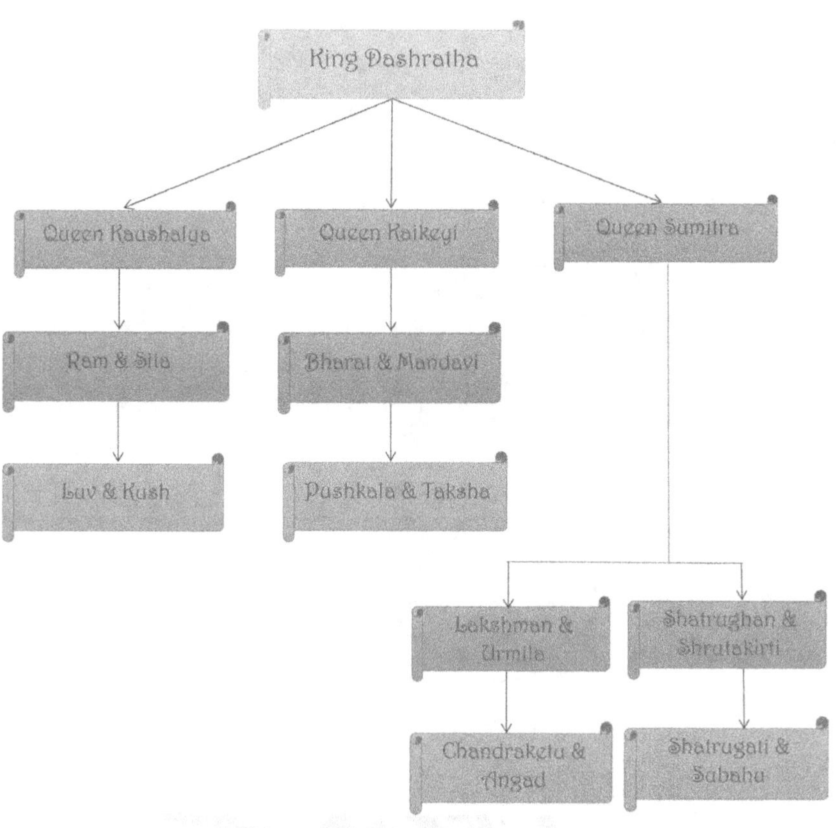

|| जय श्री राम ||